Surviving Puberty

Louise Spilsbury

Raintree is an imprint of Capstone Global Library Limited, a company incorporated in England and Wales having its registered office at 264 Banbury Road, Oxford, OX2 7DY – Registered company number: 6695582

www.raintree.co.uk
myorders@raintree.co.uk

Produced for Raintree by Calcium Creative Ltd
Edited by Sarah Eason, Rachel Blount and Robyn Hardyman
Designed by Paul Myerscough and Keith Williams
Media research by Rachel Blount
Original illustrations © Capstone Global Library Limited 2021
Production by Spencer Rosio
Originated by Capstone Global Library Ltd
Printed and bound in India
PO1020

978 1 3982 0108 8 (hardback)
978 1 3982 0110 1 (paperback)

British Library Cataloguing in Publication Data
A full catalogue record for this book is available from the British Library.

Acknowledgements
We would like to thank the following for permission to reproduce photographs: Cover: Shutterstock: Blend Images; Inside: Shutterstock: Africa Studio 42, Blend Images 14, Cassiohabib 30, CCParis 13, Chairoij 6, Cliparea/Custom Media 4, Coprid 12b, Creatistal 32, 33, Designua 21, Duplass 19b, Elena Elisseeva 39, Vladimir Gjorgiev 18, Mandy Godbehear 15, Antonio Guillem 31, Ruslan Guzov 24, Darrin Henry 8, Iordani 7, Stuart Jenner 5, Kazoka 40, Oleg Krugliak 11, Matimix 29, Monkey Business Images 35, 36, 38, Motortion Films 28, Mark Nazh 23, Oliveromg 44, Pathdoc 12t, 25, Photomak 43, PhotoMediaGroup 1, 20, Rawpixel.com 16, Jan Schneckenhaus 26, Shestakoff 9, SpeedKingz 10, 34, Suravid 19t, Szefei 45, V.S. Anandhakrishna 41, VaLiza 27, VonaUA 22, Voyagerix 17, Zurijeta 37.

Contents

Chapter 1
What is puberty?

Puberty is the time in life when your body begins to develop and change as you turn from a child into an adult. Your body fills out and changes shape as you begin to look more like your adult self.

The pituitary gland is a peanut-shaped gland at the base of the brain that releases a wide variety of hormones, some of which control growth and are important during puberty.

GLANDS ON THE GO

You do not get a say in when your body starts changing, it just happens. It starts when your pituitary gland, a pea-sized gland located at the base of your brain, releases special hormones. Hormones are chemical substances that make changes happen in the body. They travel through the blood, carrying instructions to the **cells** that make up your body. During puberty, the pituitary gland releases growth hormones that make your body and bones grow. It also triggers other glands to release different hormones, which make your body fill out and change shape. These hormones work on different parts of the body, depending on your anatomy. For example, boys' shoulders typically get broader and girls' bodies often get more curves.

Everyone has different experiences of puberty and goes through it at different rates and different times, but it's puberty that turns us from children into adults.

BE PREPARED

So if all this stuff just happens to you why do you need to know about it? Knowing about the physical and emotional changes that puberty brings, before they happen, means you know what to expect. If you are well informed you will be better prepared to deal with them. You can also plan ahead and make sure you have the stuff you will need, such as **sanitary towels** or **deodorant**, so that you are prepared.

Knowing the facts about what really happens also means you can ignore some of the silly things other kids might say about puberty if they don't understand it. Being informed also keeps you from feeling alone, confused or insecure. It helps to know that everyone, no matter who they are, where they live or what they are like, goes through puberty.

Time to change

There are no definite dates for when puberty starts and when it ends. It usually happens in the early teenage years but it happens at different times for different people. The time puberty starts also differs between boys and girls, as girls generally start earlier than boys. Most girls start puberty between the ages of eight and fifteen and most boys tend to go through it between the ages of ten and eighteen, but some people start earlier or later. It all depends on the individual. Some people get through puberty in a year or less, while for others their **adolescence** lasts for six years or more.

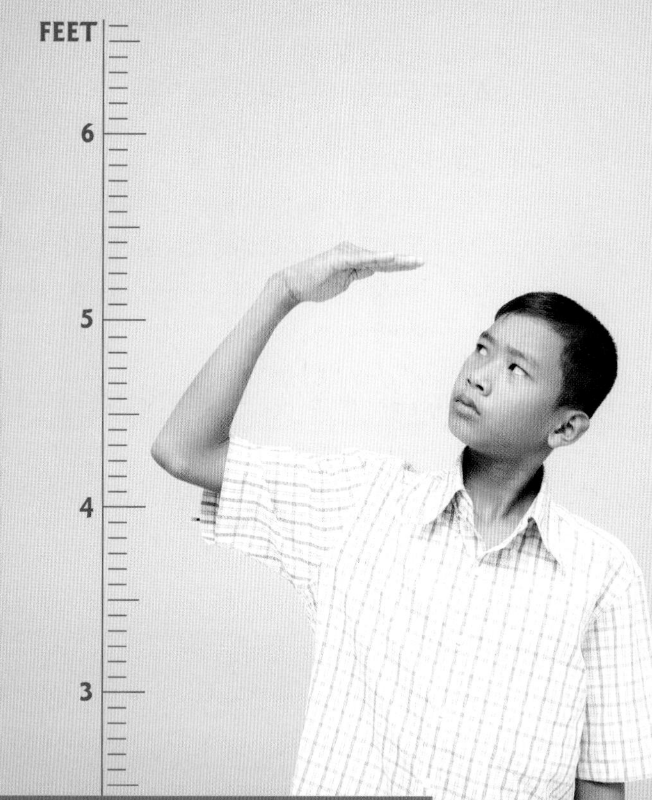

Puberty can bring dramatic changes in height in a relatively short space of time!

WHAT IS A GROWTH SPURT?

Your body has been changing from the moment you were born. In your first year of life, you had a real **growth spurt** and you grew amazingly fast. Then your growth settled down and you got taller more steadily and gradually. When you hit puberty, you have a second and final big growth spurt. Your body grows very quickly in a short space of time. When this growth spurt finishes, you will have reached your final adult height.

GROWING UP AND UP

Lots of children notice that puberty has started when their favourite jeans or skirts seem too short or when they realize that many of the girls at school are suddenly taller than most of the boys. A growth spurt lasts for about three years, and in that time girls can grow over 11 centimetres (4 inches) and boys almost 12 centimetres (5 inches). But again, people grow at different rates and to different adult heights. The final height you grow to will be affected by the height of your parents and their parents before them. That kind of stuff is **hereditary**.

People stop growing taller after they have been through puberty and reach their adult height.

Stay cool!

Puberty can be a confusing time. Some people fret that they have started puberty too early. Others feel like everyone around them is changing before their eyes and worry that puberty will never start for them. With puberty there is no one size that fits all. Everyone goes through puberty at different times and at different rates. It makes no difference if you start earlier or later, so try to stay cool. There's nothing to do but accept that and just let your body changes happen.

There is no point in worrying about whether friends are going through puberty faster or slower than you are. Puberty is different for us all.

BE GOOD TO YOURSELF

With all the changes that come with puberty, it's not surprising that it can make people feel self-conscious about their appearance. If you start changing shape, getting spots or growing facial hair earlier than other people in your class, it can feel as if everyone is looking at you. Or, if you see other people changing before you do, you may feel awkward. Remember, it's all part of growing up. There's no point in comparing yourself to other people because everyone goes through puberty at a different pace and it can be a unique experience in some ways for everyone. Try to do things that will make you feel positive about yourself. Focus on the things you do well and that you like about yourself.

Try to stay positive during puberty and appreciate the things you like about yourself.

Skills for Life

- **Think of the things you like about your appearance, such as your smile or hair. Notice these things when you look in a mirror every day.**
- **Write down five things you are really good at, such as cooking or maths, or being kind and helpful.**

- **Don't let negative thinking take hold. If a negative thought comes into your head, make an effort to replace it with something positive.**
- **Don't compare yourself to other people or to celebrities. Appreciate your body for all that it does for you.**

Chapter 2
Body challenges

The shape and size of our body changes dramatically when we grow from children into adults. In a relatively short space of time, our legs and arms get longer and our hands and feet get bigger. Muscles get bigger too, especially on boys. The way weight is distributed around the body changes too, which is what causes boys to often get broader chests and shoulders, and girls to often get wider hips and bigger breasts. Even the shape of our face changes too, often getting longer or more oval-shaped where once there were rounded cheeks.

Most girls reach their final adult height by fourteen or fifteen years of age. Most boys have stopped growing by the age of sixteen.

FEELING CLUMSY?

During this growth spurt, your body grows so quickly that the brain can have trouble keeping up. When you suddenly get taller your centre of gravity shifts higher up your body. It can take your brain a little time to readjust and work out how to balance and walk at this new height. Not only that, but your feet may also feel particularly large at the moment because they often start to grow before the rest of the body. Your hands do too, and this may make you more clumsy and awkward than usual. It's normal to find yourself tripping up or dropping things.

This is irritating, but try to remind yourself that the rest of your body will eventually catch up and you will feel less clumsy before too long. If you feel awkward, it can help to make sure you wear clothes that fit you properly. Even though you will go on growing and changing for a while, getting clothes that fit and suit your changing body can make you feel more confident and comfortable in your own skin, and help you to appreciate your new shape.

During puberty people can feel clumsy because they are more conscious of their own body and they are getting used to their rapidly changing bodies.

Sweat it out!

As you enter puberty, you will probably notice that your armpits are wetter and more smelly than they used to be, especially when it's hot or you're playing sports. This happens to both boys and girls, because puberty hormones affect our sweat glands. There are two types of sweat glands in the body and one sort, the apocrine glands, only kicks in at puberty. These sweat glands also make chemicals that can make you smell, especially when you feel nervous or anxious.

Sweat is natural and normal, and if you have a regular hygiene routine it should not cause you any problems.

Sweating is normal and useful because its helps our bodies to cool down when we get hot but sweaty armpits, hands or feet can get smelly. One way to fix that is by taking a warm shower every day. Most people shower in the morning to wash away night-time sweat. You need to use soap or shower gel all over, especially under your armpits, in your crotch and on your feet. These are the parts of the body that sweat the most and where sweat is less able to evaporate, so they can quickly start to smell. Many people shower more than once a day if they are very sweaty, after playing sports or in the summer.

If you need extra help, deodorant helps to cover up the smell of sweat under your armpits or antiperspirant can help keep your armpits dry.

MAKE A CHANGE

Keeping clean and smelling sweet isn't just about washing regularly. You also need to wear fresh underwear and other clothes after a shower because your clothes contain sweat and bacteria that smell. If you've been doing sports or any kind of activity that makes you sweat more than usual, you might also want to change your clothes more often. You could have two pairs of shoes for school and wear them on alternate days so that they have a chance to air in between. Some trainers can go in the washing machine to freshen up.

Change your socks more than once a day if you need to – for example, slipping on a fresh pair after a post-match shower.

Declare war on spots!

WHAT CAUSES SPOTS?

Your skin is covered with tiny holes called pores, which contain glands that make a substance called **sebum**. Sebum is necessary because it keeps your skin and hair moist and healthy. However, hormonal changes during puberty can make your glands produce too much sebum. When this happens, it can clog up a pore and turn into a spot.

Try to keep your skin clean to help avoid breakouts.

THE MANY FACES OF ACNE

Acne can take many forms. You may get whiteheads, blackheads or small red bumps, and they most often appear on your face, neck, shoulders and upper back. Many teenagers whose parents had acne back in the day will also get it, but other factors, such as stress and diet, can play a role too.

Depending on how bad your acne is, you may not be able to get rid of it entirely, but there are some steps you can take to reduce it. Keeping stress to a minimum can really help and part of this is making sure you get enough sleep. Drinking plenty of water and avoiding sugary foods are also good ideas.

It can seem like a conspiracy to make you miserable but spots are just a normal part of puberty!

Skills for life

- Wash your face once a day with a mild soap or cleanser.
- Choose make-up and sunscreens that are labelled "oil-free" or "noncomedogenic".

- Don't scrub too hard when you wash – it can irritate your skin.
- Don't squeeze or pop spots – you could be left with permanent scars.

Chapter 3
Girl talk

For most girls, the first sign that puberty is starting is when their breasts begin to grow. Women have breasts so that, if they have a baby, the breasts can provide the milk that is the best source of food for a newborn. During puberty, a girl's breasts grow as fat builds up around the mammary glands – the glands that are used to make breast milk.

Girls' breasts start to grow when puberty begins. They may go on growing until women are in their twenties.

BREAST CONCERNS

Breasts grow to different sizes and at different rates. Sometimes one breast grows more quickly than the other and sometimes one breast will always be just a little bigger than the other, but most of the time they even out. Some girls feel excited to see their shape changing, but others feel differently. Some feel embarrassed to be the first girl in their class to grow boobs; others worry that their breasts are too big or too small. Some worry that their nipples stick out or that they stick in. The fact is that breasts and nipples come in different shapes and sizes, and these differences are caused by the **genes** you inherit from your parents.

CHOOSING A BRA

Once a girl develops breasts, she should get a bra. Bras protect and support breasts, which is especially important when you are exercising. They also make most girls feel more comfortable. The best way to choose the right bra for your size and shape is to be fitted at a shop. It feels a bit embarrassing the first time you do it but it's important to get the right size for your breasts and your comfort. You don't want a bra that pinches or has straps that keep sliding off your shoulder. Bra sizes come in two parts. The chest or band size is the measurement around your chest in inches, such as 32, 34, etc. The cup size is for the part of the bra that holds up your breasts and is given in letters, starting with AA for the smallest. So your bra size will have a number and one or two letters in it, such as 32C or 36AA.

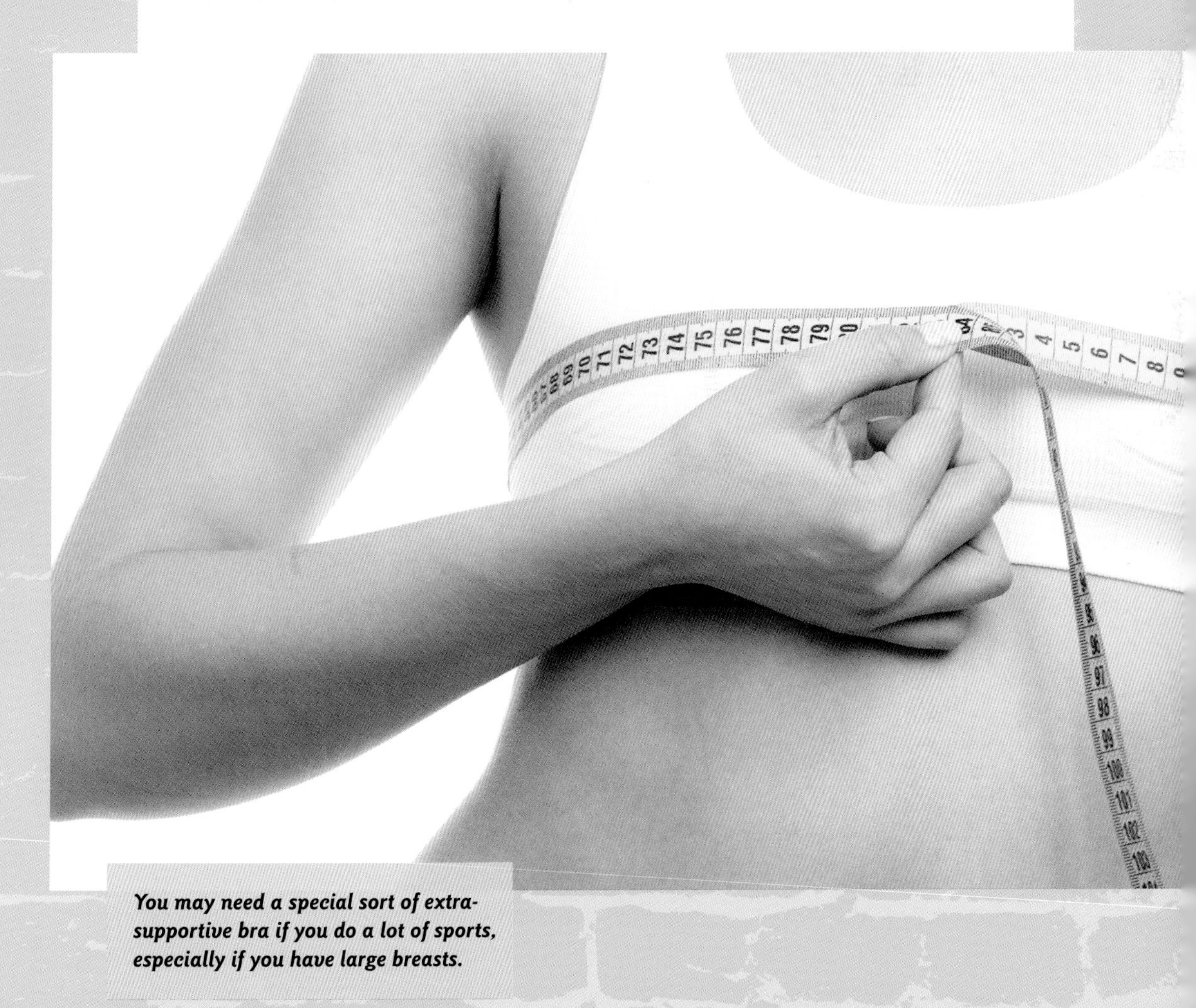

You may need a special sort of extra-supportive bra if you do a lot of sports, especially if you have large breasts.

Body hair

Another change that comes with puberty is the amount and colour of the hair on our bodies. Everyone starts to grow hair under their arms and on the **pubic regions**, which are the areas around the **genitals**. At first this hair might be quite thin and wispy and fairly light in colour. As you go through puberty it will get thicker, longer and darker. In the pubic region it also gets curly.

In some parts of the world girls and women never shave their natural armpit hair. It should be your choice whether to remove it or not.

HAIR WHERE?

Girls notice that the hair they already have, for example, on their arms and legs, is growing darker and thicker. The hair above their lips may also get a bit darker and thicker, and a line of hair may develop around their nipples and between their belly button and pubic hair. If the hair on their legs and armpits gets very long, thick or dark, some girls choose to remove it. It is a good idea to speak to your mum or another trusted adult before you try removing any body hair for the first time. They can help you to decide on the best method of hair removal.

When you wax your legs the hair takes longer to regrow.

Skills for life

- You can use a razor to shave hair from skin that is covered in soapy foam or shaving gel. The hairs will regrow quickly and can feel spiky. Shaving can sometimes irritate the skin. Never shave the hair on your face, as it will grow back thicker and darker.
- You can apply hair removal cream to the hair. This dissolves hairs at the roots so they grow back more slowly and softer. This method costs more and is messy.
- Waxing is when you apply strips of warm wax to the hairs then pull them off. The hairs come off with them. It can be painful but regrowth is slow.
- **Bleaching** or **electrolysis** are options.

- Plucking individual hairs with tweezers is painful and takes too long. Save this method for your eyebrows if you want to shape them. You should never pluck hair around the nipples as this can cause ingrown hairs and infection.

You can get hair removal wax in different forms, including pots of liquid wax like this.

What are periods?

As well as changes on the outside, girls experience changes inside their bodies during puberty. About two years after their breasts start to grow, girls get their first **period**. A period is a time of about five days, during which the body releases blood through the **vagina**. Although this sounds strange and perhaps a bit scary, periods are nothing like losing blood after you cut or hurt yourself. During a period, the body is simply getting rid of extra blood that it has made and does not need. Having periods is a sign that a girl is healthy and growing up and that her body is getting itself ready to have a baby sometime in the future.

The actual blood loss during a period does not hurt but many girls get stomach cramps or other discomfort, such as headaches.

WHY DO PERIODS HAPPEN?

Periods start when hormones from the pituitary gland trigger the two **ovaries** in a girl's body to start making another hormone called **oestrogen**. These hormones start a girl's **menstrual cycle**. There are thousands of **eggs** in the ovaries, and each ovary is attached to the **uterus**, or **womb**, by a pipe called a fallopian tube. The menstrual cycle starts when one of the ovaries releases an egg into its fallopian tube, so the egg can travel into the uterus. Before the egg is released, the lining of the uterus swells with extra blood and **tissue**. If the egg is **fertilized** by a **sperm** while inside the uterus, it starts to develop into a baby. The extra blood and tissue protects and nourishes the baby as it grows.

Most of the time, however, the extra blood and tissue in the uterus lining is not needed because the egg is not fertilized. It therefore passes out of the body through the vagina. This flow of blood-like fluid is what we call a period. A period can last for anything from two to seven days. About two weeks after the last day of a period, a new egg is released and the menstrual cycle starts again.

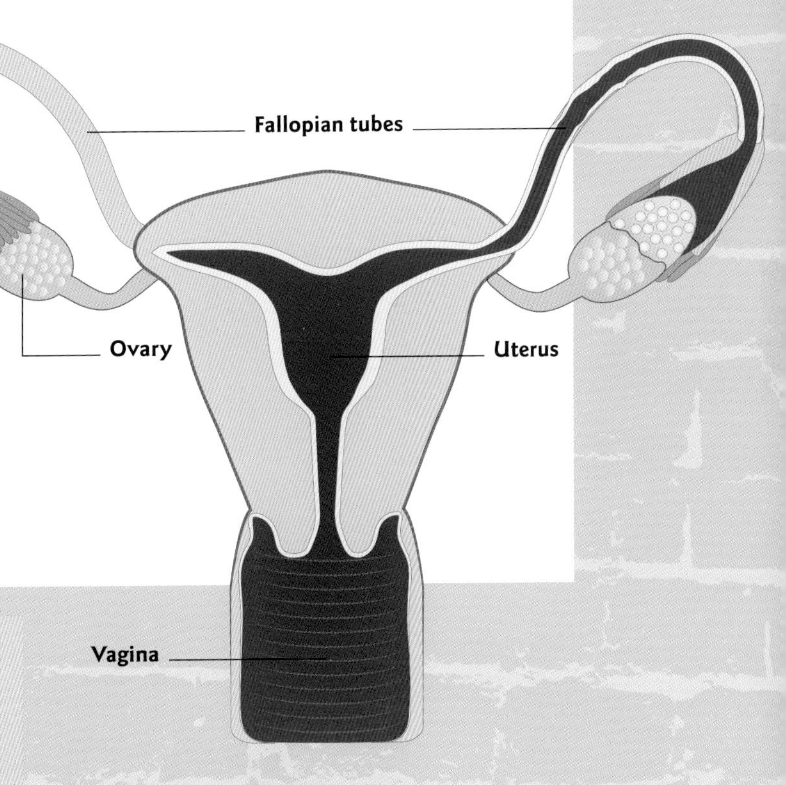

These are the body parts involved in menstruation. The uterus is about the size of a plum and the ovaries are about the size and shape of unshelled almonds.

Coping with periods

During a period, girls need to use a sanitary towel or a **tampon** to soak up the menstrual blood. Sanitary towels are absorbent pads that have a sticky strip that attaches to the inside of pants. A tampon is a small, crayon-shaped cotton pad with a string at one end. It goes inside the vagina and the string hangs outside, so you can pull it out after it has done its job. There are instructions on the box for how to use tampons or you can ask an older female friend or relative to explain.

If you make a note of when a period begins, it will help you to know roughly when to expect the next one in the following month, so you can be prepared.

CHANGING PADS AND TAMPONS

Sometimes the blood flow is heavier at the beginning of a period and lighter towards the end. You can get thicker pads and bigger tampons for heavier days. You can also get panty liners, which are very thin pads, for the end of a period. It is very important to change your pads and tampons regularly: at least once every four hours. Tampons can cause a rare but serious medical condition called **toxic shock syndrome** if they are not changed regularly. Your periods may come a little irregularly to begin with, so it's a good idea to keep clean underwear and some sanitary towels with you in case you get caught out and a period starts earlier or goes on longer than expected.

You may not feel like exercising sometimes during a period, but stretching and gently working out can really help with stomach cramps.

PERIOD PROBLEMS

Premenstrual syndrome, or PMS, is when changing levels of period hormones affect a girl's mood and make her feel upset, irritable or tired. If this affects you, try to avoid stress at these times, get plenty of sleep and do something nice to relax like taking a warm bath. Another problem is that girls sometimes get headaches, stomach cramps, sore breasts or back pain during their period. Exercise and stretches may help, and a hot water bottle can sooth stomach cramps. If you need painkillers, check with an adult first.

Chapter 4
Boys' bodies

When boys hit puberty, hormones from the pituitary gland travel through the blood to the **testes** glands. The hormones cause the testes to start producing a hormone called **testosterone**. Testosterone is responsible for many of the changes that turn a boy into a man. For example, it makes boys' voices deepen and makes extra body hair grow.

While a boy's higher voice is changing into the deeper voice of a man, it can crack, break and warble suddenly, even in the middle of a song.

CHANGING VOICES

At some point during puberty, boys notice that their voice suddenly changes halfway through a word or sentence. They might have a high, squeaky voice one minute and a low, deep voice the next. Some boys find that their voice sounds really croaky and strange for a while. That is because their voice is starting to get the deeper tones of a man. The human voice comes from throat muscles called vocal cords, which are found in the **larynx**, or voice box. During puberty the larynx grows and the vocal cords get longer and thicker. As the body adapts to these changes, a boy's voice cracks or squeaks unexpectedly. This can be annoying and sometimes boys get teased about it but it is perfectly normal and it usually only lasts a few months.

WHAT IS AN ADAM'S APPLE?

Another surprising change boys will notice is that they grow an Adam's apple. An Adam's apple looks like a big bump moving up and down on the front of a man's neck when he swallows. It develops because a boy's larynx grows so much during puberty and tilts to a different angle, making it stick out at the front of the throat. A girl's larynx grows and her voice deepens a little during puberty too, but not as much as a boy's.

The larynx bump at the front of the throat is called an Adam's apple, after the story in the Bible about Adam in the Garden of Eden eating a piece of the forbidden fruit, which gets stuck in his throat.

Who is that in the mirror?

When you are going through puberty there are so many changes going on that you may be surprised by what you see in the mirror. For one thing, hair starts to sprout all over the place! Boys grow hair on their chest, legs, face, armpits and pubic region. Whether you have lighter, darker, thicker or thinner hair growth is all down to your genes. Most boys do not need to do anything about this hair growth at first because it starts off light and fine. When it starts to grow more thickly, you may want to start shaving your face. It's a good idea to talk to your dad or caregiver about shaving before you do it for the first time.

As your body changes and gets hairier, taller and broader you may not feel you recognize yourself in the mirror sometimes!

GET IT OFF YOUR CHEST!

Most boys see their shoulders grow wider and their body become more muscular. Some boys worry that they are not as muscly as their friends but, like everything else in puberty, the rate of change varies in scale and time. Just try to eat healthily and exercise regularly and your body will fill out as it is supposed to. Another thing some boys notice is a small amount of breast growth on their chest. Again, this is nothing to worry about. It is normal and will settle down as your body grows and changes. It will probably go away by the end of puberty.

Skills for life

- **An electric razor is easy to use to shave your face and pretty effective, although it does not give as close a shave as a manual razor.**
- **To use a manual razor, you cover your beard area with shaving cream or gel first. This makes the shave easier and prevents irritation.**

- **Avoid sharing shavers or razors, as this can spread infection.**

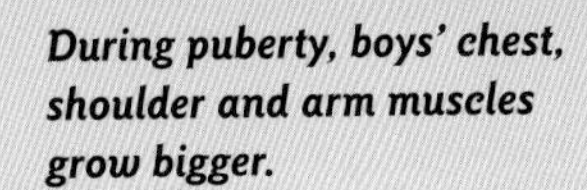

During puberty, boys' chest, shoulder and arm muscles grow bigger.

Boys only

As boys go through puberty, their genitals and **reproductive organs** change. The testicles get bigger and the **penis** gets thicker and longer. Try not to worry about your size or compare yourself to others. Testicles may grow at different rates but they even out eventually, and it is common for one testicle to hang a little lower than the other. Testicles also start producing sperm, which will one day be able to join with and fertilize a woman's egg to start a baby growing.

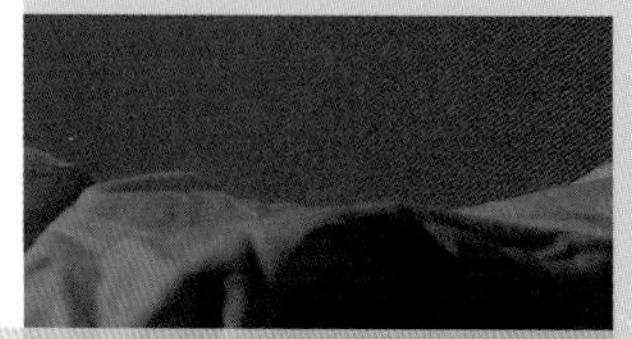

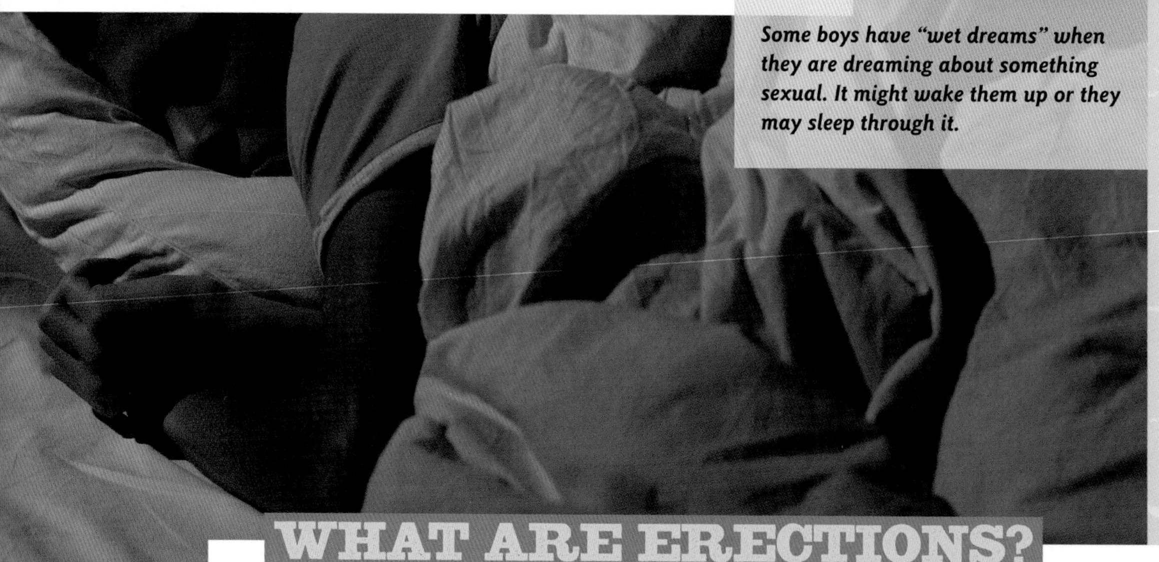

Some boys have "wet dreams" when they are dreaming about something sexual. It might wake them up or they may sleep through it.

WHAT ARE ERECTIONS?

During puberty, boys also start to have **erections**. Erections happen when **blood vessels** in the penis widen to let in more blood, making the penis bigger, stiffer and point upwards. When an erection happens, boys may also **ejaculate**. That is when sperm travels up the tubes inside the penis and out of the end. The sperm and fluids that come out of the penis are called **semen**. After ejaculation, or when an erection is over, the blood vessels in the penis narrow again and things return to normal.

AVOIDING EMBARRASSMENT

Boys often start to get sexual feelings around this time and they may start **masturbating**, when they touch their penis to make it grow and ejaculate. They may also have "wet dreams", when they ejaculate in their sleep. Erections can happen unexpectedly, which can be embarrassing, though it is unlikely that other people will notice. To stop an erection, try thinking about a boring task like counting backwards from a hundred! As you pass through puberty these things will happen less and you will be able to control erections.

The testicles are inside a sac of skin called the scrotum that hangs outside the body. This keeps them cool but also means they can get hurt easily. Protect them with a sports cup when necessary.

Chapter 5
Ups and downs

Have you ever been on a rollercoaster? One minute you're going up and the next you're hurtling down at terrifying speed? That is what puberty can feel like sometimes because it brings not only physical changes but big emotional changes too. These feelings partly happen because oestrogen and testosterone hormones affect the way you feel as well as the way your body looks. They also happen because of the changing responsibilities and challenges that come with becoming more independent.

Going through puberty can be like a rollercoaster ride as your emotions go up and down. You'll feel great sometimes and low other times, but the ride will end!

WHY DO I FEEL LIKE THIS?

Of course you have emotions before puberty, but during puberty your emotions can feel so much more intense. You may find that things make you much more angry, sad, happy or excited than before. Not only do your emotions get stronger, they also change more frequently and suddenly. So one minute you can feel fine and the next you might feel like crying. These mood swings can make you feel out of control. They can lead to arguments or conflicts with friends and family too.

FEELING BETTER

Although it's not your fault that you feel up and down, there are things you can do to make life a little easier. Try explaining to people when you're feeling tired, cross and unable to talk, and put off conversations until later. Talk to a good friend or an adult, sharing with them how you feel. Also, try making time to relax, exercise and do the things that make you feel good. You could keep a journal of your feelings. Expressing things like this can let some of the emotion out. Most importantly, remind yourself that this won't last forever. Your brain will learn how to deal with these emotions and get better at reading other people's emotions too.

Remember that you are not alone, and not the only one dealing with difficulties. The chances are that even people who look like they've got it together probably feel the same as you do!

Parent problems

As teenagers grow, they start to form their own opinions and may want to spend more time with friends. They start to become more independent; they want more control over their lives and to make more of their own decisions. They may question their family's rules and ideas and this can lead to conflicts with parents. Some parents worry their children will take unnecessary risks, so they stop them from going out or they get angry when their teen seems moody or doesn't want to join in family activities. When you're going through puberty, it can often feel as if you are always arguing with your parents or that they simply don't understand you.

However frustrating your family might be at times, losing your cool won't help!

HOW TO IMPROVE FAMILY RELATIONS

It can help to remember that parents only ask questions and make rules because they care. The way the brain develops and changes during puberty does make some teenagers take risks, thinking that nothing bad could happen to them and then they do get hurt. Your parents will know this can happen, so because they don't want you to come to any harm they may be stricter than you think is necessary. In any conflicts with your parents it will really help if you can keep calm, be honest about how you feel and try to find compromises. That means finding a solution that you can both accept.

Skills for life

- Make a mind map of ways to **compromise** with your parents.

Going out

- Tell parents where I'm going and who I'm going with.
- Give parents my friends' home addresses and phone numbers.
- Agree on a time to come home.
- Text or call if I'm late or change plans.

Communication

- Try to explain my point of view.
- Listen to what they have to say as well.
- Keep calm and try not to shout.

COMPROMISE

Home Life

- Agree to finish all homework before going out.
- Make schedules for schoolwork.
- Do chores without complaining to prove I am mature and capable.

Figuring out ways to compromise with your parents can improve family relations.

Friends and dates

Heart racing, palms sweating, butterflies in your stomach? During puberty, there are some people you know or see whom you suddenly start to feel strongly about. Having a crush on someone like this is a normal part of growing up. This starts to happen at different times for different people, so don't worry if you are not interested in dating anyone or meeting someone special just yet. Lots of people are happy just hanging out with friends, concentrating on schoolwork or hobbies and doing the things they enjoy. Eventually you may find someone who makes you go weak at the knees. What will be, will be.

WHY DO I FEEL LIKE THIS?

Some people have a crush on a celebrity, someone in their class or a person they see on the bus but have never spoken to. Lots of people feel a little funny when they talk to or are near their crush. They may feel tongue-tied, red in the face and shy. For some people, the reason they get a crush on someone is that sex hormones in their body are becoming more active, making them interested in people in a way they have never experienced before.

Falling for someone can be emotional and can make you happy or sad and angry too.

CONTROLLING A CRUSH

Being happy and content is all about keeping a balance. Thinking about your crush is fine but don't let it become an obsession that stops you from doing other things you enjoy.

It can be exciting to have a crush on someone, and it can help you to figure out the kind of person you would like to be with as you get older. If they like you too, you may even go on dates with them. But when emotions are running high like this it is easy to get hurt: for example, if your crush starts seeing someone else or rejects you. It's important to keep these feelings in perspective and not to let them rule your life. Don't spend so much time daydreaming that you stop having fun with your friends and family, doing schoolwork and all the other things you usually do.

Chapter 6
Survival guide

Going through puberty can be challenging and tiring, but there are lots of things you can do to survive it and to make sure you stay happy and healthy!

STRESS BUSTERS

If you're feeling stressed, one of the first things to do is to figure out what is triggering that feeling. Then you can either avoid those triggers or do something about them. For example, if getting all your homework done on time or studying for an exam is worrying you, draw up a schedule and stick to it. That way, you will feel in control and able to concentrate on one thing at a time instead of worrying about everything all at once. If there are particular activities that worry you, like speaking in class, you could also try some calming deep **breathing exercises**. Practising speaking in front of a mirror or family and friends can help you get over your anxiety.

Getting organized and getting work done on time can reduce stress.

EXPRESS YOURSELF!

Teenagers have a lot going on. You probably have lots of schoolwork and chores at home, and you want to spend time with your friends too. But try to fit in time to do the creative things that give you pleasure. Perhaps you like singing, performing or painting? These are great outlets for stress and for letting your feelings out. Some people like to keep a diary, or journal, every day. They write about what happened and how they feel about it. Venting your feelings like this can really help.

Exercise is good for your body and your mind! It makes you stronger and helps you to relax.

HOW DOES EXERCISE HELP?

Exercise helps in several ways. Being active keeps you fit, keeps you from gaining too much weight, helps you to look good and even helps you to feel happier and less stressed! Exercising releases chemicals in your brain called **endorphins** that help improve your mood, so find some kind of physical activity that you enjoy. It doesn't have to be a sport; dancing can be just as good for you as running. Ideally, try to get half an hour to an hour's exercise every day.

Talk about it

Lots of young people have anxieties or questions about puberty and growing up. Some feel excited and look forward to becoming more independent. Others worry about the new changes and wish they could go back to being a child when everything seemed simpler. These are perfectly normal feelings, and most people will feel both at one time or another. It really helps to talk about how you feel. Bottling up your emotions can make you feel more alone and anxious.

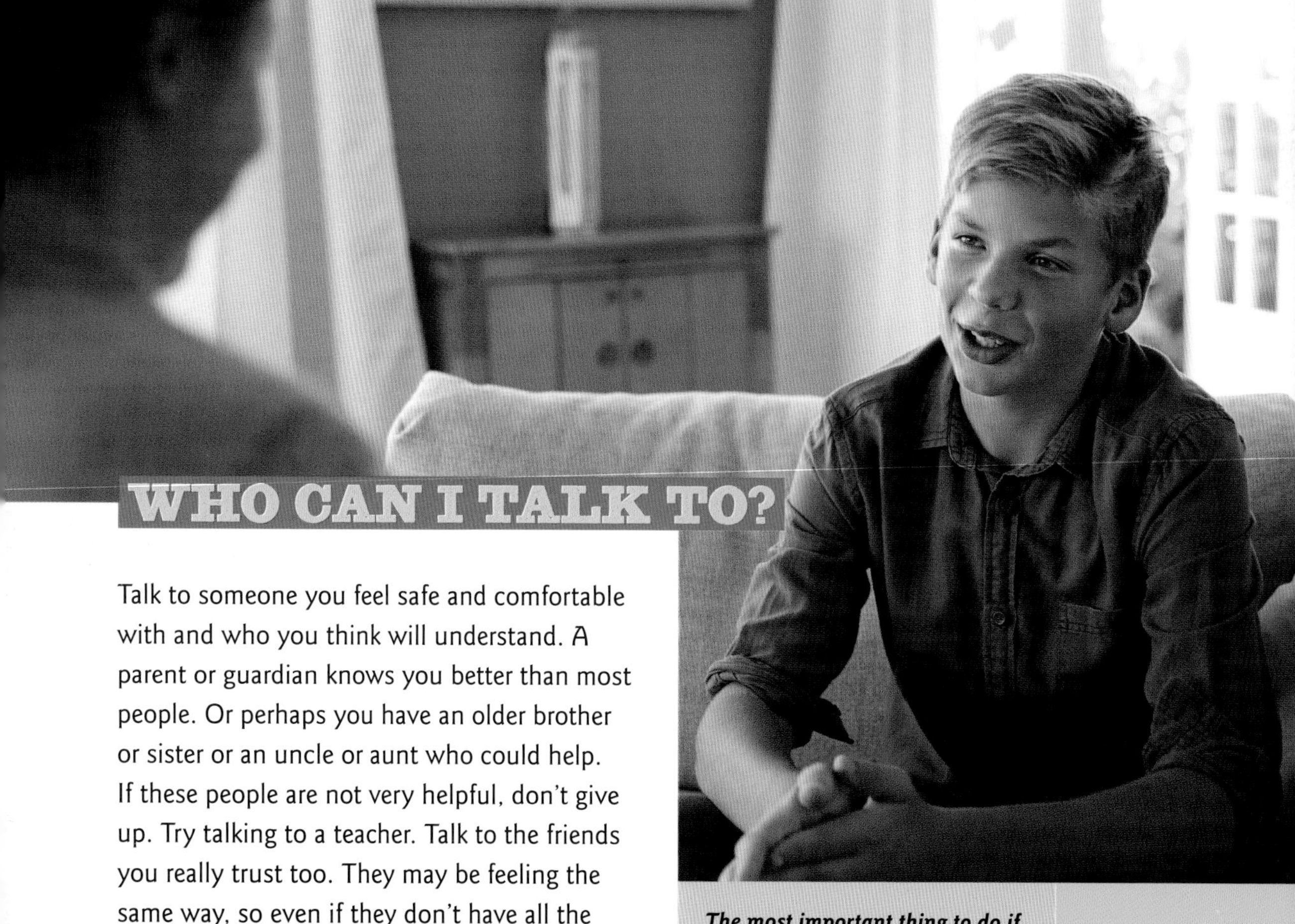

WHO CAN I TALK TO?

Talk to someone you feel safe and comfortable with and who you think will understand. A parent or guardian knows you better than most people. Or perhaps you have an older brother or sister or an uncle or aunt who could help. If these people are not very helpful, don't give up. Try talking to a teacher. Talk to the friends you really trust too. They may be feeling the same way, so even if they don't have all the answers, sharing your feelings with them can help you.

The most important thing to do if you have any worries or concerns about puberty is to talk about it.

Skills for life

If you have something difficult to say or you are angry about something and need to explain your feelings to someone, try **role-playing** it with a friend first. They play the person you have a problem with or need to talk to, and you play yourself. You can ask them to pretend to be angry or uninterested so you can rehearse calmly saying what you feel. For example, if they act like a parent who keeps saying they have no time to talk, you can role play explaining why you need their time and how you want them to listen to you calmly and openly, without getting angry.

Role-playing is great for preparing for all kinds of situations.

Keeping healthy

Do you feel hungry all the time? That's not unusual during puberty because your body is doing a lot of growing and developing, and food is the fuel that powers this growth. The important thing is not to satisfy your hunger with junk food. It is more important than ever to eat healthily. That means eating lots of fruit and vegetables, some protein and filling up on **carbohydrates** like pasta and rice. If you need a snack, reach for a piece of fruit rather than crisps and chocolate.

Try to drink plenty of water too. Lots of your bodily functions require water, and your cells need water to work properly. Not drinking enough water can cause tiredness, headaches, dry skin and even make it harder to concentrate and do your schoolwork.

Getting into a habit of eating a variety of healthy foods and drinking plenty of water while you're young can help you to look good and stay well for the rest of your life.

WORRYING ABOUT WEIGHT

During puberty, weight distribution around the body changes. It is normal and healthy for people – most often girls – to become curvier and gain some weight. As this is also the time when almost every young person is thinking more about how they look, some people start to worry that they are getting overweight and feel uncomfortable about how their bodies are changing.

If you are worried about your weight, ask your parents or doctor for advice. Many teens who think they are fat are actually well within a normal weight range for their height. Unless your doctor says you have a weight problem, it is unhealthy to diet or skip meals. Just try to get into good eating habits and exercise regularly.

As you get older you will have more chances to buy your own snacks and meals, away from home. It can be tempting to choose all the things your folks have warned you not to eat too much of, but do your body a favour and keep treats to a minimum. Make healthy choices instead and you'll stay a healthy weight!

Time for bed

The growth spurt and other changes you go through during puberty can make you feel full of energy some days but exhausted on other days. Never underestimate the power of sleep! At this important stage of your growth and development, you need more sleep than adults. Sleep helps us to learn and remember things and to feel alert and able to concentrate. Lack of sleep affects your mood; being tired can make you feel more irritable or sad. You should aim for at least eight to nine hours of good sleep each night. If you find you always want to sleep late at the weekend to catch up or you fall asleep in the day, you may need even more.

Making sure your bedroom is dark, cool, quiet and comfortable can help you get off to sleep.

WHAT IF I CAN'T GET TO SLEEP?

Sometimes we find it hard to get to sleep, even when we are really tired. Getting regular exercise helps with this. It is also helpful to get into a regular routine, at least in the week during school time. That means going to bed at a regular time and doing the same things before you go to sleep, such as taking a warm bath, reading or listening to music. Avoid eating too much or too little close to bedtime so that you do not feel too full or hungry.

It's important to avoid using mobile phones, tablets or other screens for at least an hour before bedtime. Switch them off so they don't buzz or flash while you're trying to get to sleep. Many scientists believe that the light from these devices blocks the natural effects in the brain that make us feel sleepy.

Doing the same things in the same order for an hour or two every night before you settle down in bed can help you drift off to sleep.

Loving life

There are ups and downs during adolescence and lots of challenges to deal with, but this is also an incredibly exciting time in your life. You are becoming more independent, and you can make more of your own choices. You and your friends can go out and try new experiences. Make the most of the interesting opportunities that come your way, such as school trips or the chance to meet new friends. Enjoy family times, whether that means singing along while you do chores or sharing a laugh with parents and siblings. Make the most of your life!

Spending time outside, seeing nature and getting fresh air puts problems into perspective, makes us feel more relaxed, gives you more energy and even sharpens the mind!

RELAX!

One thing that can really help you to love life is learning how to relax properly. Relaxing does not just mean sitting around, it means switching off from the day's activities and doing different things, including things you enjoy. So try new activities or do more of the things you love. It doesn't matter how good you are at them, just doing them will give you a boost of confidence. Getting outdoors, seeing the world and getting some fresh air also make us feel good.

Try something new! Learning a new skill is immensely satisfying and relaxing and can make you feel really good about yourself.

Skills for life

Do not let bad feelings build up. If there is something worrying you, such as whether the changes in your body are normal, go and see a doctor about your concerns. They will be able to put your mind at rest. If you are struggling with really bad emotions, ask to see a counsellor. Talking to a professional can help you learn how to deal with these emotions in a healthy way.

Glossary

acne a skin condition that causes spots on the face and other parts of the body

adolescence the time in a child's life when they go through puberty and become an adult

antiperspirant a substance used to prevent or reduce sweat

bleaching using a special substance that can make dark hair look lighter

blood vessels tubes through which blood travels around the body

breathing exercises breathing in deeply and slowly through the nose and breathing out slowly through the mouth

carbohydrates a type of food that gives the body energy

cells the basic units that make up all living things

compromise when two sides agree to give up some of their opposing demands to meet somewhere in the middle

deodorant a substance used to mask the smell of stale sweat

eggs the female sex cells that can develop into babies if fertilized by sperm from a man's body

ejaculate when semen comes out of the end of the penis after an erection

electrolysis the removal of hair on the skin using an electric current

endorphins hormones that can trigger a positive, happy feeling in the body

erection when a boy's or man's penis becomes larger and stiffer

fertilized when a male sperm joins with a female egg inside her body, and the egg starts the long process of developing into a baby

genes the parts passed from parent to child that provide instructions about what the child will look like

genitals the external sexual organs of the body

gland a body part that makes and releases hormones that tell parts of the body how to behave, such as when and how to grow

growth spurt when the body grows quickly in a relatively short period of time

hereditary describes characteristics that children inherit from their parents

hormones the body's chemical messengers

larynx the part of the throat that contains the vocal cords that give us our voice

masturbating touching one's genitals for sexual pleasure

menstrual cycle the cycle of changes that happen from the first day of a woman's period to the day before her next period

oestrogen a female sex hormone

ovaries the female body parts that produce eggs and female sex hormones

penis the male sex organ

period a time in the menstrual cycle of about five days during which the body releases blood through the vagina

premenstrual syndrome (PMS) emotional changes that many girls and women go through just before a period

pubic regions the area around the genitals or external sex organs

reproductive organs the body parts that can be used to reproduce, or make babies

role-playing acting out a situation before it happens to practise dealing with it

sanitary towels pads of soft material worn inside pants to absorb menstrual blood

sebum an oily substance made and released by glands in the skin

semen a milky fluid produced by male sex organs to carry sperm

sperm the male sex cell that can fertilize an egg inside a woman's body

tampon a plug of soft material that can be inserted into the vagina to absorb menstrual blood

testes (singular **testicle**) plum-shaped glands inside the scrotum that make sperm and male sex hormones

testosterone the male sex hormone

tissue groups of similar cells that work together to do a specific job, such as skin cells that form skin tissue

toxic shock syndrome an infection that can be caused by wearing a tampon for too long

uterus the part of a woman's body in which a baby can develop

vagina the tube that leads from a girl's or a woman's uterus to the outside of the body

womb another word for the uterus

Find out more

BOOKS

Girlology: Body Pro: Facts and Figures About Bad Hair Days, Blemishes and Being Healthy, Erin Falligant (Raintree, 2019)

Growing Up: Humans from Birth to Old Age, Dr Jen Green (Raintree, 2019)

The A-Z of Growing Up, Puberty and Sex, Lesley De Meza (Franklin Watts, 2014)

What's Happening to Me? (Boys Edition) (Facts of Life), Alex Frith (Usborne Publishing Ltd, 2013)

What's Happening to Me? (Girls Edition) (Facts of Life), Susan Meredith (Usborne Publishing Ltd, 2015)

WEBSITES

BBC Bitesize
www.bbc.co.uk/bitesize/clips/zxxcd2p
This BBC Bitesize video explains the dramatic changes that take place during puberty.

Childline
www.childline.org.uk
Childline offers advice and support for children.

Kids Health
kidshealth.org/en/kids/puberty.html
KidsHealth offers information and advice about puberty.

Note to parents and teachers: the Publishers have made every effort to recommend websites that are from trustworthy sources and that are age-appropriate for the readers of this book. However, due to the changing nature of the internet, we cannot be responsible for content shown on these pages and we recommend that all websites are viewed under the supervision of a responsible adult.